Brain-Boosting
Visual Logic Puzzles

LAGOON
BOOKS

Series Editor: Heather Dickson

Puzzle Contributors: Anna Claybourne,
Rich Garner, David King, Colin Russ

Additional Contributors: Joel Hilshey,
Roya Ireland, Peter Sorenti

Page Design and Layout: Linley Clode

Cover Design: Gary Inwood Studios

Published by:
LAGOON BOOKS
PO BOX 311, KT2 5QW, UK
PO BOX 990676, Boston, MA 02199, USA

www.lagoongames.com

ISBN: 1902813200

Printed in Thailand

Brain-Boosting Visual Logic Puzzles

Introduction

Just as going to the gym tones your body and enhances your level of fitness, doing puzzles hones your brain and therefore boosts your IQ.

With this thinking in mind, we have compiled one of the best cerebral workouts ever.

Within this beautifully illustrated book we have brought together nearly 100 of the best visual logic puzzles – that is puzzles that have a crucial visual element that you have to work out using reason and logic. We have then sorted them into chapters:

In **Chapter 1** – you will find the easiest puzzles – ones you should really be able to complete within 60 seconds.

In **Chapter 2** – you will find a slightly more difficult set of puzzles – ones you should complete in three minutes.

In **Chapter 3** – you will find a much more difficult range of conundrums, which should take about five minutes to crack.

And in **Chapter 4** – you will find the most fiendish puzzles that could take up to ten minutes to work out. At what level you decide to exercise is entirely up to you.

You can dip into the book whenever you want but for the more competitive reader, why not decide which level of puzzles you wish to tackle then turn to the chapter and work your way through the puzzles?

Each puzzle has been rated 1 - 3. So as long as you crack each puzzle – within the time limit allocated in each chapter – you can award yourself the relevant points. We have provided a helpful scoring card after each chapter heading, in order to help you keep score in each chapter.

For the ultimate challenge, total the points you score in each chapter and turn to page 191 to see how you fared overall – a score of 128 or more is the absolute proof of a true academic Adonis.

For those of you who want to test the theory that practice makes perfect, why not jump to the last chapter of the book and see how you fare? If you find the puzzles easy, then you really are a puzzle genius. If you do not, however, then go back to the beginning of the book and do the puzzles in chronological order. This time, when you get to the puzzles in Chapter 4 you should have no excuses – your score should have leapt up after all the practice!

If by the end of the book, you have still not achieved your ultimate cerebral goal and you want more practice, then turn to page 192 to see Lagoon's other Brain-Boosting titles.

Contents

Chapter 1

To score points in this chapter, you need to provide the correct solution to each puzzle within 60 seconds.

To see individual ratings for each puzzle look under the title of each question. Once you have completed the chapter, turn to page 8, for help adding up your score.

Then turn to page 53 to start chapter 2.

Chapter 1 - Scoring

Puzzle points for correct answer

Doodle Mania	...... **1**	Enigma	.... **2**
Headspin	.... **3**	Plus Totals	.... **1**
Triominoes Triangle	... **3**	Caterpillar Caper	.... **1**
E Block	.... **2**	Square Numbers	..... **2**
Night Shift	.... **1**	Triangle Tricks	...... **2**
Train Tracks	.... **1**	Metal Links	.... **2**
Shape Shifting	...... **2**	Roulette Run	.... **1**
Diamond Maze	...... **2**	Linear Labyrinth	..... **2**
Bouncing Ball	.... **1**	Curious Cubes	.... **1**
Puzzle Pieces	.... **3**	Colour Conundrum	... **3**
Twosome	.... **3**	Square Search	.... **1**

YOUR TOTAL

/ **40**

Doodle Mania

Rating 1 Point

Starting from the left-hand-side of this maze
make your way between the squiggles until
you find a path across to the other side.

Doodle Mania - Solution

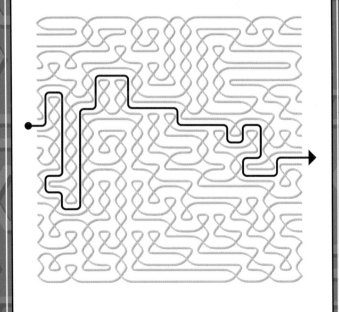

Headspin

Rating 3 Points

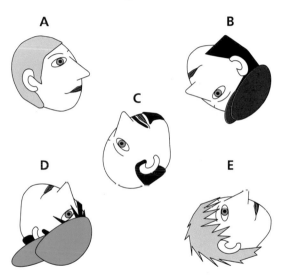

A

B

C

D

E

Which of these heads
is the odd one out?

Headspin - Solution

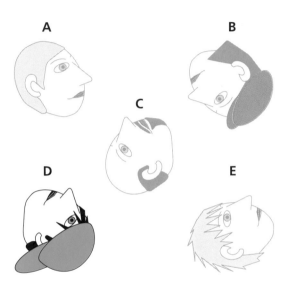

A B C D E

When rotated the right way up,
D is facing left; the others are facing right.

Triominoes Triangle

Rating 3 Points

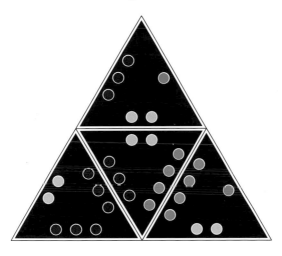

Four triominoes may be put together in a number
of different ways, with their matching edges having
the same number of spots, to form a larger triangle.
In the example shown the total of the spots on
the outside of the large triangle is 12.
For those four triominoes what is the maximum
possible total of the spots on the outside?

Triominoes Triangle - Solution

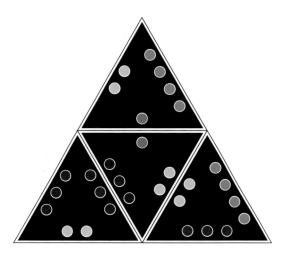

18. The total of all the spots is 30. Putting the triomino
with only 6 spots in the middle the total of all
the inner spots must be 12, leaving 18 on the outside.
One of the arrangements is shown above.

E Block

Rating 2 Points

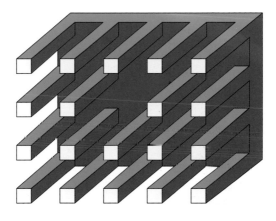

What is the maximum number of Es that can be cut out from this piece of wood without dissecting any of the prongs?

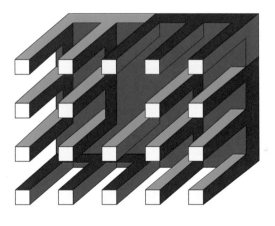

6, as shown.

Night Shift
Rating 1 Point

Shaun's shifts at the shirt factory
seem to be at random times, but as his
boss points out, there is a pattern.
What time will Shaun's next shift start?

Night Shift - Solution

Each time take the time shown and add
that number of hours to get the next time.

Train Tracks

Rating 1 Point

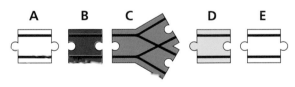

Grant's daughter Eve asks him to help her build her toy railway. She wants to make one track split into two. Grant needs four of these five pieces to complete the track. Which one doesn't he need?

Train Tracks - Solution

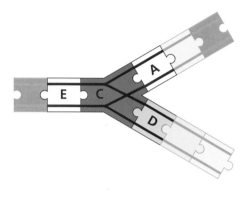

He doesn't need B.

Shape Shifting
Rating 2 Points

is to

as

is to **?**

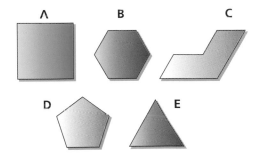

A   B   C

D   E

Shape Shifting - Solution

 is to

as  is to

B. The shape is doubled along its longest edge.

Diamond Maze

Rating 2 Points

Try to work your way through the
spaces around the diamonds to get
from the top to the bottom of this maze.

Diamond Maze - Solution

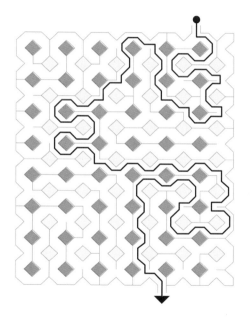

Bouncing Ball

Rating 1 Point

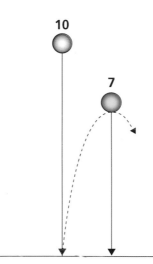

A ball is dropped from a height of 10 feet
and bounces up to a height of 7 feet. Assuming
that the recovered height after bouncing continues
at the same rate, after how many more
bounces will the ball be below 2 feet?

Bouncing Ball - Solution

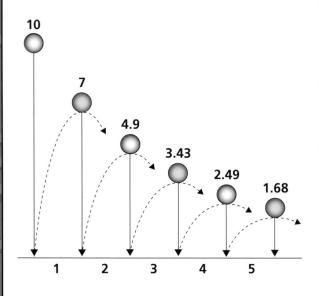

After a further 4 bounces as shown above.

Puzzle Pieces

Rating 3 Points

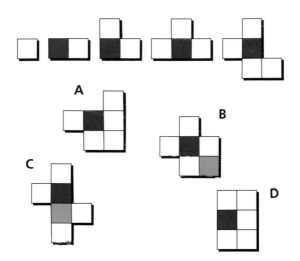

Gepetto is cutting pieces for a puzzle.
Each piece he cuts is one square bigger than the
last piece. What will the next one look like?

27

Puzzle Pieces - Solution

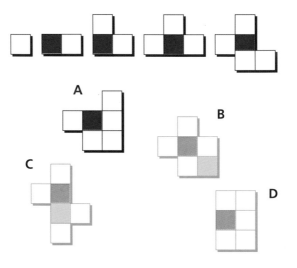

Each time, the previous shape is
rotated 90 degrees anti-clockwise and a new
square is added on the bottom right.

Twosome

Rating 3 Points

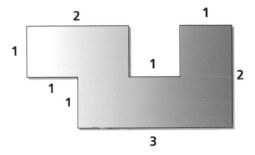

2

1

1

1

1

2

1

1

3

What is the smallest number of these identical shapes that are needed to make two complete squares, without any protruding edges?

Twosome - Solution

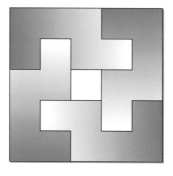

4, as shown.

Enigma

Rating 2 Points

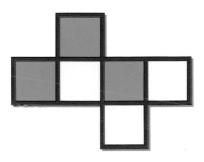

E N I G M A

Arrange the six letters of the word ENIGMA on
this plan in such a way that, when it is folded up
into a dice, the letters that are next to each
other in the word are next to each other on the dice,
but letters that are immediate neighbours in the
alphabet are not next to each other on the dice.

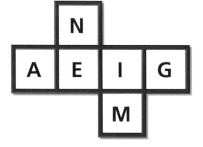

Plus Totals

Rating 1 Point

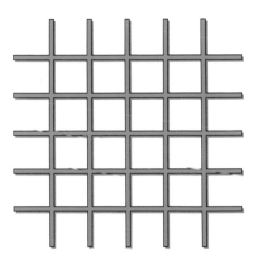

A plus (+) has equal arm lengths.
How many are there in the diagram?

Plus Totals - Solution

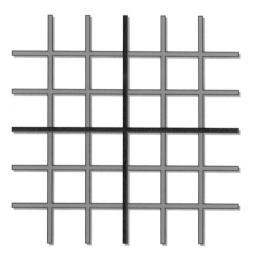

Where 1 is the largest size and 5 is the smallest,
there are 25 (size 5) plus 9 (size 4) plus 9 (size 3)
plus 1 (size 2) plus 1 (size 1) which gives a total of 45.

Caterpillar Caper

Rating 1 Point

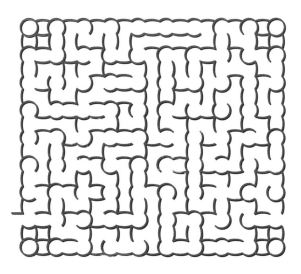

In this maze you must move from
the entrance at the left, through the broken
circles, to find a route to the exit on the right.

Caterpillar Caper - Solution

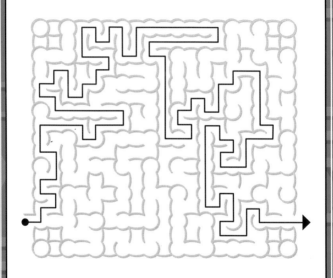

Square Numbers

Rating 2 Points

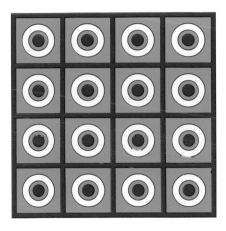

How many different squares can
you find in this 4 x 4 grid?

Square Numbers - Solution

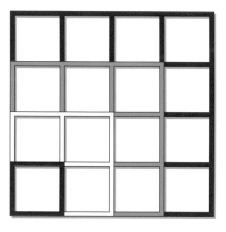

There are 30 different squares.
From largest to smallest:
1 plus 4 plus 9 plus 16.

Triangle Tricks
Rating 2 Points

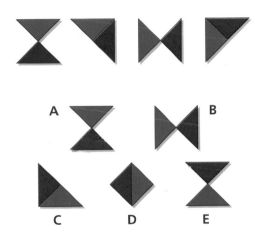

Which of the options here
continues the sequence at the top?

Triangle Tricks - Solution

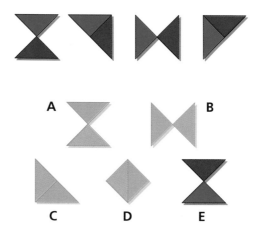

First the red triangle moves 90 degrees
anti-clockwise, then the blue triangle,
then the red triangle and so on.

Metal Links

Rating 2 Points

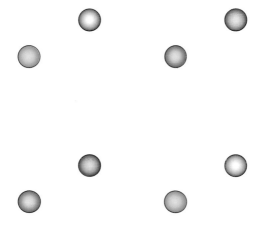

Eight balls are positioned on the corners of an
imaginary cube. Each ball is connected to every
other ball by a metal rod. How many rods are there?

Metal Links - Solution

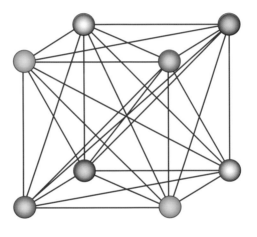

There are 28 rods altogether.
(Each ball has 7 rods attached to it,
so 7 + 6 + 5 + 4 + 3 + 2 +1 = 28).

Roulette Run

Rating 1 Point

01

11

22

34

When Rachel plays roulette on the rickety roulette wheel at Raffles, she notices something strange about the numbers that come up. If the sequence continues, what number should Rachel bet on next?

Roulette Run - Solution

01

11

22

34

47

The first digit follows the sequence
0, 1, 2, 3, 4, etc. The second digit is always the
sum of the two digits of the previous number.
The numbers also increase each time by
a set amount: first 10, then 11, then 12.
To continue the sequence, 13 must be added to 34.

Linear Labyrinth

Rating 2 Points

Try to find your way from the left of this maze
to the right. There is only one correct path.

Linear Labyrinth - Solution

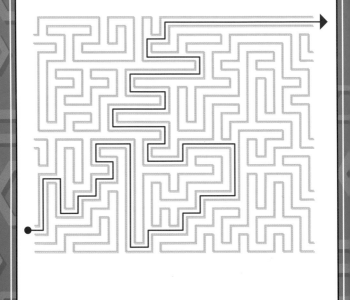

Curious Cubes

Rating 1 Point

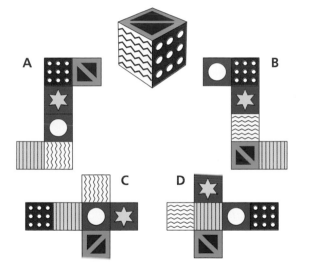

Only one of these flat plans will fold up to
make the dice shown. Which one?

Curious Cubes - Solution

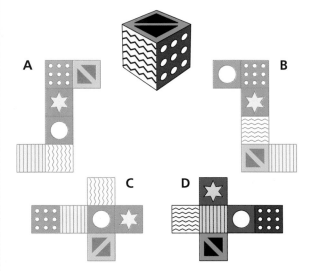

A

B

C

D

Colour Conundrum

Rating 3 Points

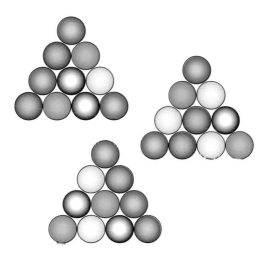

20 lottery balls, 4 of each colour, are stacked together in the form of a regular tetrahedron. The three side views of the stack are shown. What is the colour of the ball that cannot be seen?

Colour Conundrum - Solution

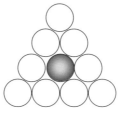

The ball in the middle of the bottom layer is blue.

Square Search

Rating 1 Point

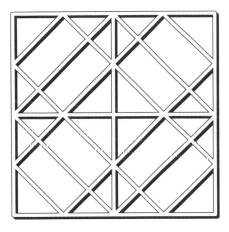

How many squares can you
count in the grid above?

Square Search - Solution

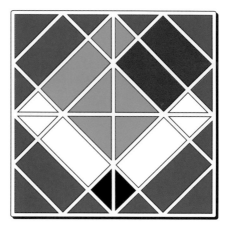

From largest to smallest:
1 plus 1 plus 4 plus 5 plus 4 equals 15.

Chapter 2

To score points in this chapter, you need to provide the correct solution to each puzzle within three minutes.

To see individual ratings for each puzzle - look under the title of each question. Once you have completed the chapter, turn to page 54, for help adding up your score.

Then turn to page 99 to start chapter 3.

Chapter 2 - Scoring

Puzzle points for correct answer

Shape Up **2**

Arbour Puzzle **3**

Mobile Mystery **2**

All Squared **2**

Bubble Maze **2**

Pink Poser **1**

Take your Pick **2**

Numeral Nightmare . . **3**

On the Beach **2**

Brain Storm **1**

Pig Pen **1**

The Matrix **1**

Naming the Baby **1**

Handle with Care **2**

Cogs and Wheels **1**

Rhombuses Galore . . . **2**

Illuminations **3**

Invisible Spots **1**

Cube Routes **2**

Beatrice's Beanbag . . . **1**

Mower Cable Calculator . **3**

Burger Bar Dilemma **2**

YOUR TOTAL

/ **40**

Shape Up

Rating 2 Points

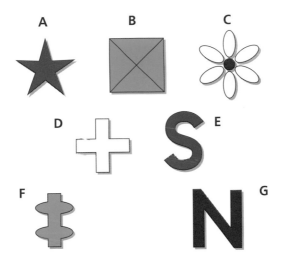

A
B
C
D
E
F
G

Which of these shapes is the odd one out?

Shape Up - Solution

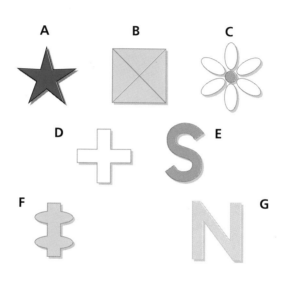

A

B

C

D

E

F

G

It's the only one that is not
the same upside-down.

Arbour Puzzle

Rating 3 Points

Show how eight trees can be planted
in six rows of three trees each.

Arbour Puzzle - Solution

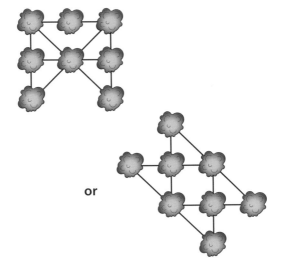

or

Mobile Mystery
Rating 2 Points

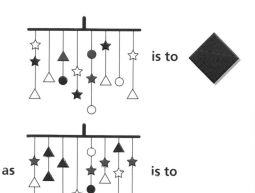

is to

as is to

A   B   C   D   E

Mobile Mystery - Solution

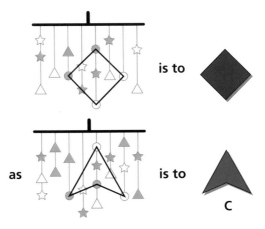

is to

as

is to

C

The answer is the shape made by
joining the circles in the mobiles together.

All Squared

Rating 2 Points

A square piece of wood has sides of 4 feet. With just two cuts create 4 equal pieces that will make a square with 5 foot sides.

All Squared - Solution

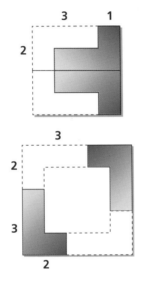

The 4 pieces are cut out and
put together as shown above.

Bubble Maze

Rating 2 Points

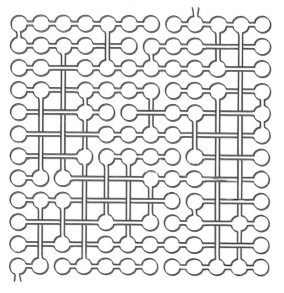

Find a path from the top to the bottom
of this maze. You can only change direction
in a bubble. When you are in a pipe, you must
keep going straight until you hit a bubble.

63

Bubble Maze - Solution

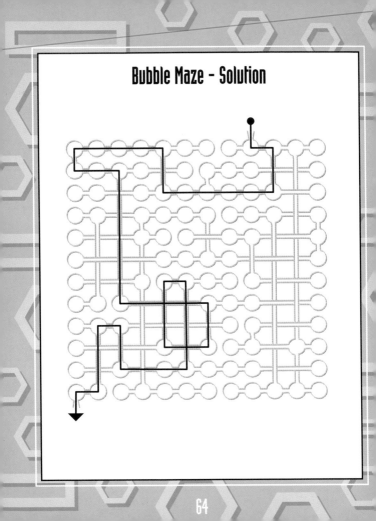

Pink Poser

Rating 1 Point

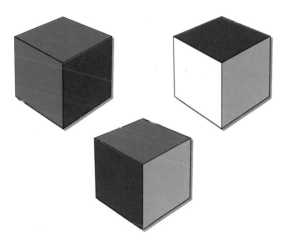

These three pictures show the same cube from different angles. Which colour is opposite pink?

Pink Poser - Solution

Green.

Take your Pick

Rating 2 Points

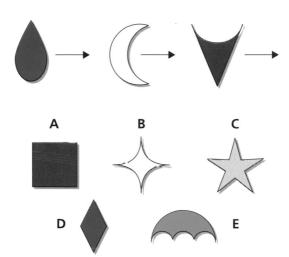

A

B

C

D

E

Most of the shapes above could be used to complete this sequence. Which one couldn't?

Take your Pick - Solution

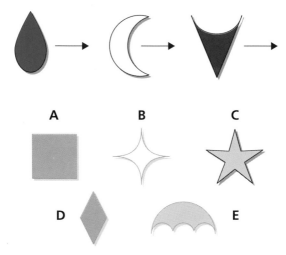

The shapes in the sequence have 1, 2 and 3 points.
C has five points, the rest have four.

Numeral Nightmare

Rating 3 Points

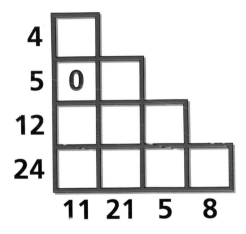

Place the digits 1 to 9 (0 as shown) in the boxes so that they add to the totals shown against each row and column.

69

Numeral Nightmare - Solution

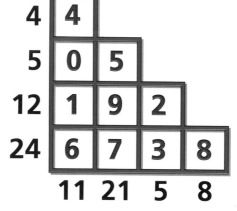

	4			
4	4			
5	0	5		
12	1	9	2	
24	6	7	3	8
	11	21	5	8

On the Beach

Rating 2 Points

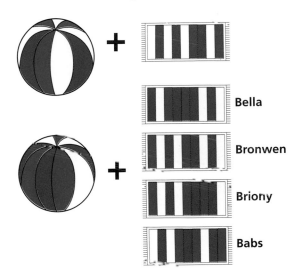

Bella

Bronwen

Briony

Babs

Like everyone else on holiday in the resort of
Neurotica, Bill has a beach ball that matches his towel.
Bill finds a lost beach ball on the beach.
Who is the owner?

On the Beach - Solution

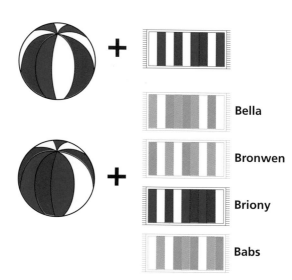

Bella

Bronwen

Briony

Babs

Briony. The sequence of colours on the towel follows that running clockwise around the beach ball, starting from the back.

Brain Storm

Rating 1 Point

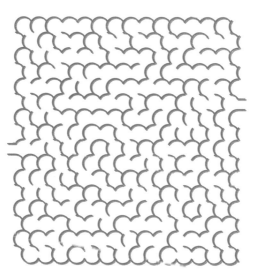

Enter this maze on the left and
move through the spaces until you
find a way out on the right.

Brain Storm - Solution

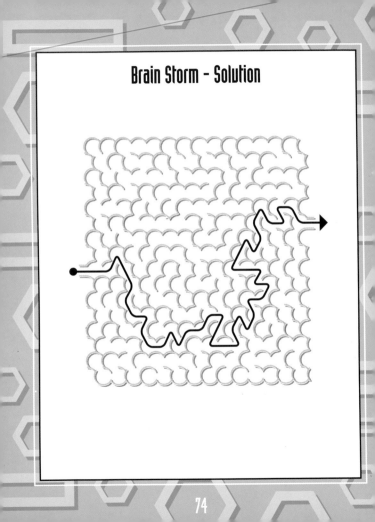

Pig Pen

Rating 1 Point

Patrick the pig farmer's pigs are kept in this polygonal pigpen with eight sections. Patrick wants to replace the fencing around all the sections. Can he travel around the whole pen, replacing the fencing as he goes, without stopping and without going along the same stretch of fence twice?

Pig Pen - Solution

The Matrix

Rating 1 Point

What's the missing number?

The Matrix - Solution

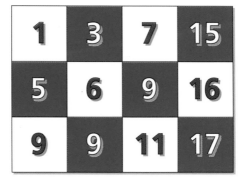

Running down the first column, the numbers go up
by increments of 4; down the second column by
increments of 3; down the third column by increments
of 2, and down the fourth column by increments of 1.

Naming the Baby

Rating 1 Point

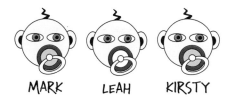

MARK   LEAH   KIRSTY

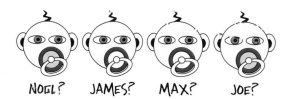

NOEL?   JAMES?   MAX?   JOE?

Alex and Zoe are about to have their
fourth baby - a boy. Their existing children are
called Mark, Leah and Kirsty, what should they
call him to complete the sequence?

Naming the Baby - Solution

JOE

Joe. The initial letter moves backwards
through the alphabet; the second letter
moves forwards through the vowels.

Handle with Care

Rating 2 Points

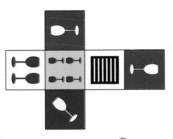

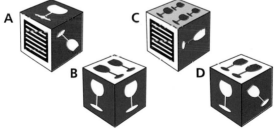

William has designed a flatpack box for the hand-blown wineglasses he sells. Which of the boxes above is not a box of William's wineglasses?

Handle with Care - Solution

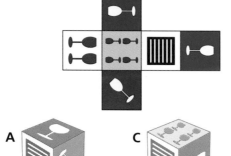

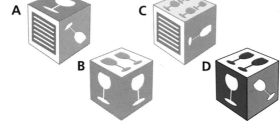

Cogs and Wheels

Rating 1 Point

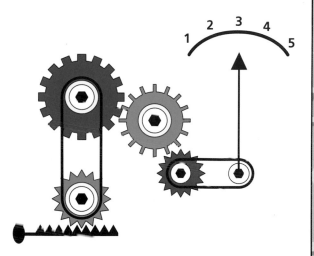

When Pete presses the plunger, is he cranking
the machine up or slowing it down?

Cogs and Wheels - Solution

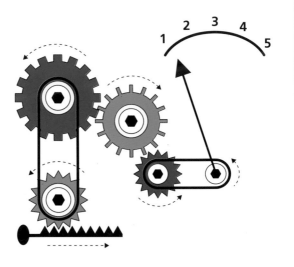

Slowing it down.

Rhombuses Galore

Rating 2 Points

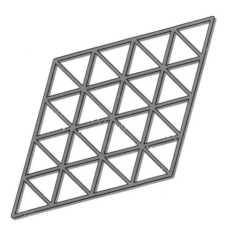

How many rhombuses can
you see in the diagram?

Rhombuses Galore - Solution

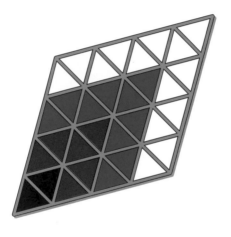

Where 4 is the largest rhombus and 1 is the smallest, there are 1 (size 4) plus 4 (size 3) plus 15 (size 2) plus 40 (size 1), which equals 60.

Illuminations

Rating 3 Points

Judy and Jay witness an alien landing. They see a series of flashing lights. What pattern will appear next in the row of lights if the sequence continues?

Illuminations - Solutions

A pattern of two lights on, one light off
is moving outwards from the centre.

Invisible Spots

Rating 1 Point

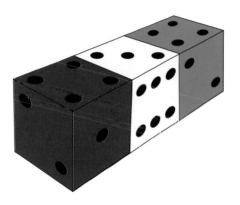

What is the total value of the spots on the
sides of the dice you cannot see in this picture?

Invisible Spots - Solutions

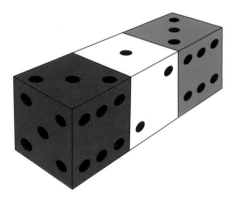

41. Each dice has 21 spots altogether. 3 x 21 = 63.
You can see 22 spots so 41 must be invisible.

Cube Routes

Rating 2 Points

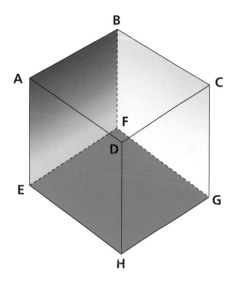

How many different routes are there from any one corner to its diametrically opposite corner? Routes must not pass twice through the same point.

Cube Routes - Solution

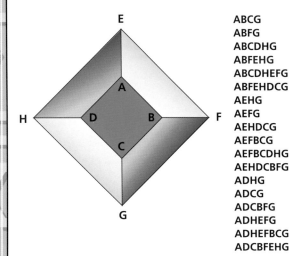

ABCG
ABFG
ABCDHG
ABFEHG
ABCDHEFG
ABFEHDCG
AEHG
AEFG
AEHDCG
AEFBCG
AEFBCDHG
AEHDCBFG
ADHG
ADCG
ADCBFG
ADHEFG
ADHEFBCG
ADCBFEHG

There are 18 possible routes, as shown.

Beatrice's Beanbag

Rating 1 Point

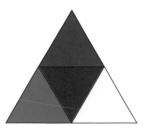

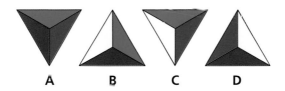

A   B   C   D

Beatrice makes a beanbag out of the piece of cloth shown here. Which of the four pictures above does not show Beatrice's beanbag?

Beatrice's Beanbag - Solution

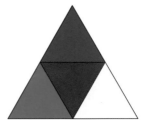

A   B   C   D

Mower Cable Calculator

Rating 3 Points

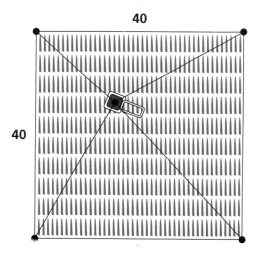

An automatic lawn mower is attached to small posts at the four corners of a square lawn (40 feet by 40 feet) by 4 cables. The cable length is controlled and kept taut by a computer inside the mower and this enables it to determine its position and cut every blade of grass. What is the approximate maximum length of cable that is ever exposed?

Mower Cable Calculator - Solution

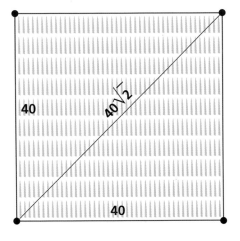

136.6 feet. This will occur when the mower is in one of the corners, and is approximately the sum of the two sides of the lawn plus its diagonal, i.e. 40 plus 40 plus 40 $\sqrt{2}$ feet.

Burger Bar Dilemma

Rating 2 Points

A   B   C   D

Bert is proud of his artistically arranged
burgers, stacked to order in a secret sequence.
What will his next burger look like?

Burger Bar Dilemma - Solution

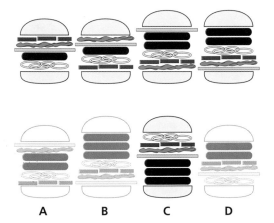

A **B** **C** **D**

An extra burger is added every other time.
Meanwhile the five ingredients - burger, cheese, lettuce,
tomato and onion - cycle upwards through the layers.

Chapter 3

To score points in this chapter, you
need to provide the correct solution to
each puzzle within five minutes.

To see individual ratings for each puzzle -
look under the title of each question.
Once you have completed the chapter, turn
to page 100, for help adding up your score.

Then turn to page 145 to start chapter 4.

Chapter 3 - Scoring

Puzzle points for correct answer

Snakes and Ladders	**3**	Magic Squares	**3**
Romantic Delusions	**3**	Vegetarian Option	**2**
Propeller Problem	**2**	Gertrude's Garden Gnomes	**1**
Jigsaw Maze	**2**	Blueberry Muffin	**2**
Changing Shape	**1**	Dice Dilemma	**1**
Laguna Traffic Lights	**3**	Find the Mascot	**2**
Cube Count	**1**	Pentagonal Poser	**3**
Overlap	**2**	Star Maze	**1**
Brainbender	**2**	Tile Torment	**2**
Tea Turmoil	**2**	Lucky Number	**2**
Floral Confusion	**3**	Dancing Feet	**2**

YOUR TOTAL

/ **45**

Snakes and Ladders

Rating 3 Points

One snake and one ladder still need to be added to this board. Which squares should they run to and from?

Snakes and Ladders - Solution

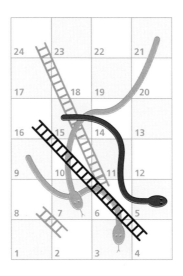

A snake should run down from square 15 to 5 and
a ladder should run up from square 4 to square 16.
Even numbers have ladders running up
to 4 x their value. Odd numbers have snakes
running down from 3 x their value.

Romantic Delusions

Rating 3 Points

Draw three straight lines anywhere on this box to make four sections, each containing two hearts, two rings and four daggers.

Romantic Delusions - Solution

Propeller Problem

Rating 2 Points

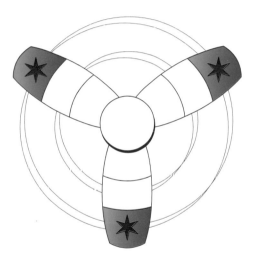

Place the seven numbers 664 to 670 on
the blades of the propeller and on the central
axis so that there is a total of 2001 along
each blade and around each ring.

Propeller Problem - Solution

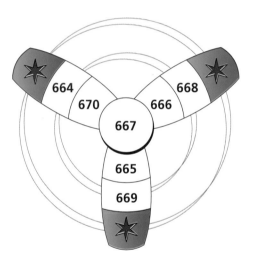

Jigsaw Maze

Rating 2 Points

Travel from the top row of this puzzle to
the bottom row, moving from one jigsaw piece to
the next. You can only enter or exit a puzzle piece
if it interlocks with the puzzle piece you are on.

Jigsaw Maze - Solution

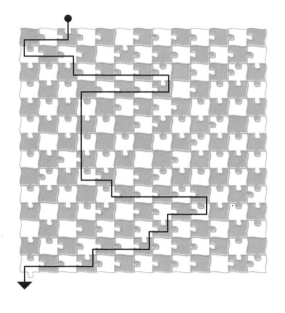

Changing Shape
Rating 1 Point

is to

as

is to

A

B

C

D

Changing Shape - Solution

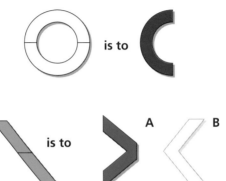

is to

as 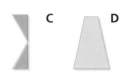 is to

A   B

C   D

The shape is folded along the line
and rotated 90 degrees.

Laguna Traffic Lights

Rating 3 points

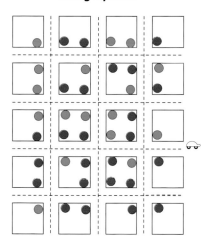

In Laguna, the traffic control system requires cars,
all driving on the left-hand-side of the road, to turn
left at the next junction for a green light and right
for a red light. Lights are on the driver's left-hand-side.
If there is no light, cars go straight on at the junction.
After being passed, the light changes colour
from red to green and vice versa. The map shows a
car leaving the system. Where did it enter?

Laguna Traffic Lights - Solution

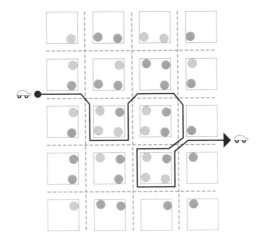

It entered and took the route as shown
(lights back to their original colours)

Cube Count

Rating 1 Point

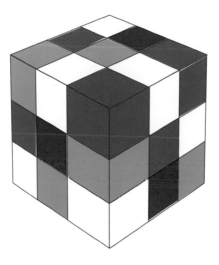

How many different cubes are
there in this 3D cube?

Cube Count - Solution

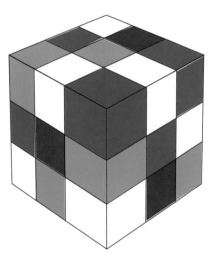

There are 36 different cubes.

Overlap

Rating 2 Points

Two pieces of paper overlap each other on
a table. The corner of the smaller piece of paper lies
at the centre of the larger sheet of paper.
What proportion of the larger piece is overlaid?

Overlap - Solution

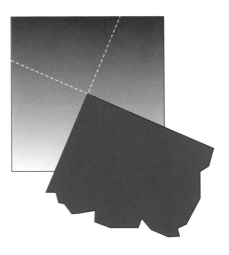

The dotted lines show that a quarter of the underlying piece of paper has been covered up.

Brainbender

Rating 2 Points

Brian wants to try a new Brainbender cocktail, but he's trying to keep his alcohol units down and he has no idea exactly how much alcohol there is in a Brainbender. However, he has the above clues.
How many glasses of wine should Brian forgo in order to have a Brainbender instead?

6 glasses of wine.

Tea Turmoil

Rating 2 Points

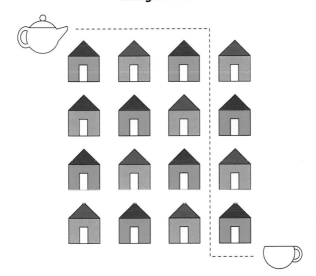

To get to the teacup, the teapot can be
carried along streets going downward or to
the right - as the route shows. How many different
routes, in all, are there to the cup?

Tea Turmoil - Solution

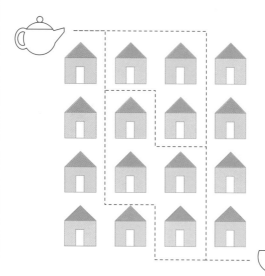

There are 35 different routes - three are shown above.
The matter is related to a mathematical cornerstone:
Pascal's Triangle. But simple counting gives the answer.

Floral Confusion

Rating 3 Points

If Fran's flowers go in this vase –

– which vase should Veronica put hers in?

A   B   C   D

Floral Confusion - Solution

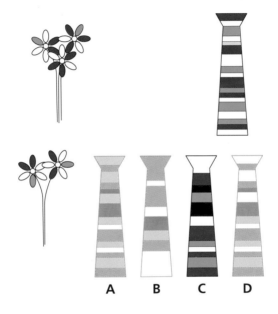

The number of stripes on the vase
represents the number of petals.
The arrangement of the stripes is irrelevant.

Magic Squares

Rating 3 Points

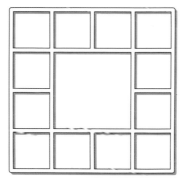

1, 2, 3, 4, 5, 6,
7, 8, 9, 10, 11, 12

Place the numbers 1 to 12 in the squares so that there is a total of 22 along each edge.

Magic Squares - Solution

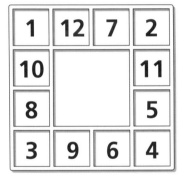

There are several solutions but all have
1, 2, 3, and 4 at the corners.

Vegetarian Option

Rating 2 Points

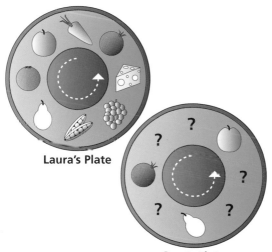

Laura's Plate

Sam's Plate

Laura and Sam have plates that are almost identical, with the same eight vegetables laid out on the plates as above. However, none of the vegetables on Sam's plate is next to the same vegetables on Laura's plate. On Sam's plate, the peas are still two places behind the cheese. What vegetable is immediately in front of the tomato?

Vegetarian Option - Solution

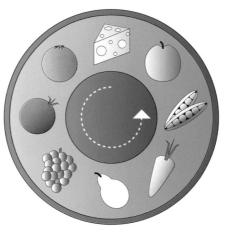

Sam's Plate

The grapes.

Gertrude's Garden Gnomes

Rating 1 Point

Gertrude already has four garden gnomes in a row by her pond. To complete the sequence, which type of gnome should she choose from the garden centre's selection?

Gertrude's Garden Gnomes - Solution

A   B   C   D

The colour sequence red, yellow, blue, red, green cycles downwards through the five areas of gnome clothing: bobble, hat, top, trousers, boots.

Blueberry Muffin

Rating 2 Points

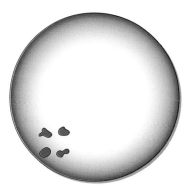

You would like to share this blueberry muffin fairly
with a friend, but the blueberries have been unusually
positioned. By making just three straight cuts with a
knife, can you cut the muffin into two pieces of equal
size and shape, each with two blueberries on top?

Blueberry Muffin - Solution

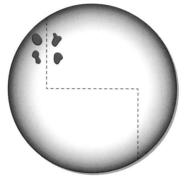

Dice Dilemma

Rating 1 Point

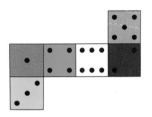

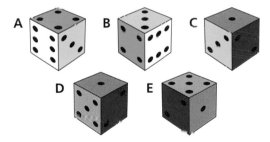

Which of these dice has been made
out of the template above?

Dice Dilemma - Solution

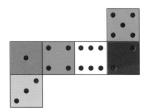

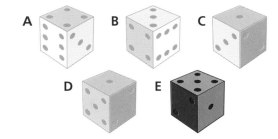

Find the Mascot

Rating 2 Points

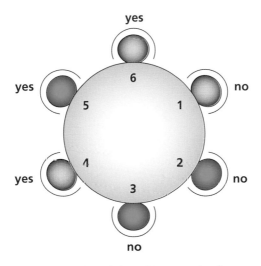

Three red guards and three blue guards of Laguna sit down to lunch. One of them has the regiment mascot beneath his chair. Either all the red guards tell the truth and all the blue guards lie or vice versa, but we do not know which. When asked the question, "Is the mascot under a chair next to you?" the guards responded as indicated. Where is the mascot?

Find the Mascot - Solution

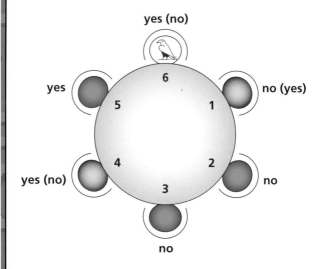

The mascot is under chair 6 –
the blue guards told the truth.

Pentagonal Poser

Rating 3 Points

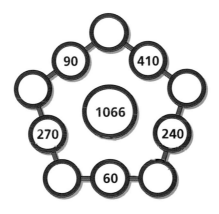

Put a whole number in each of the five empty circles so that the three numbers along each side add up to the central figure.

Pentagonal Poser - Solution

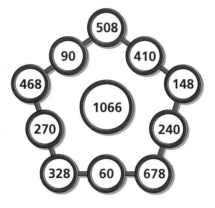

Star Maze

Rating 1 Point

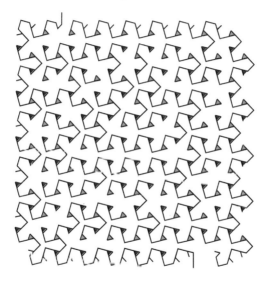

Travel through the space between
the lines to find a path from the top
of this maze to the bottom.

Star Maze - Solution

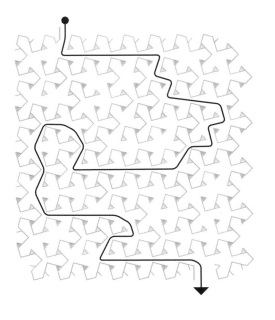

Tile Torment

Rating 2 Points

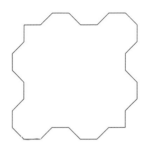

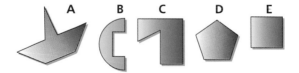

Thelma is at the tile shop. "None of these types
of tiles will cover my kitchen floor on their own,"
she sighs. In fact, she will need to use two of
these five types of tile together to cover
the floor with no gaps. Which two?

Tile Torment - Solution

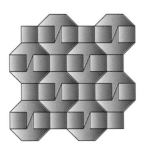

A   B   C   D   E

Lucky Number

Rating 2 Points

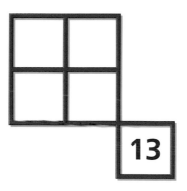

13

The diagram shows four boxes with a fifth box showing 13, the total of the whole numbers to be placed in the four boxes, e.g. 1, 3, 4, 5. In how many ways can the four boxes be filled with DIFFERENT whole numbers that add to 13?

Lucky Number - Solution

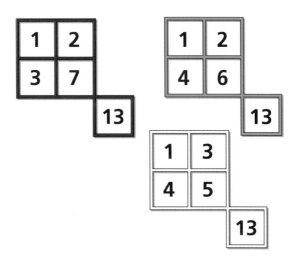

The only possibilities are the sets: 1, 2, 3, 7,
and 1, 2, 4, 6 and 1, 3, 4, 5; surprisingly few.
As the four digits in each set can be arranged in 24
different ways, the total number of ways is 72.

Dancing Feet

Rating 2 Points

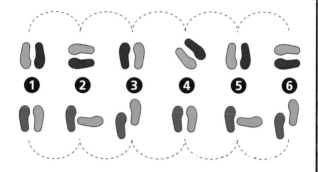

Ted and Ginger, ballroom dance champions, are
trying out an unusual new dance. Step 1 shows
the starting position. On which step will they
both be in the starting position again?

Dancing Feet - Solution

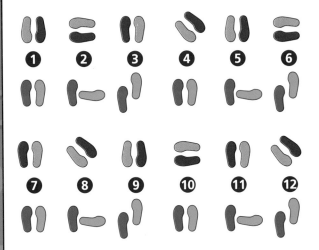

Step 13. Ted has to complete his 3-step routine
4 times (12 steps) and Ginger has to complete her 4-step
routine 3 times (12 steps). The step after that, they are
again both facing each other with their feet together.

Chapter 4

To score points in this chapter, you need to provide the correct solution to each puzzle within ten minutes.

To see individual ratings for each puzzle - look under the title of each question. Once you have completed the chapter, turn to page 146, for help adding up your score.

Then turn to page 191 to see how you fared overall in the Brain-Boosting Visual Logic challenge.

Chapter 4 - Scoring

Puzzle points for correct answer

Wondrous Windows	. . **3**	Bathroom Tiles	. . . . . . **3**
Mat-imatics	. . . . **2**	TV Crew	. . . . **3**
Cosmic Coins	. . . . **2**	Number Chain	. . . . **2**
All Aboard	. . . . **3**	Pathfinder Puzzle	. . . . **2**
Parachute Drop	. . . . . . **1**	Odd One Out	. . . . **3**
Against the Odds	. . . . **2**	12-Card Turnover	. . . . **1**
Weights in the Wood	**1**	Maple Mystery Maze	. . **2**
Ray of Light	. . . . **1**	Egg Box Enigma	. . . . . **3**
Arrow Maze	. . . . **2**	Cup Challenge	. . . . **2**
Circular Computations	**2**	Field Work	. . . . **1**
Jigsaw Jewel	. . . . **1**	Houndstooth Maze	. . . **3**

YOUR TOTAL

/ **45**

Wondrous Windows

Rating 3 Points

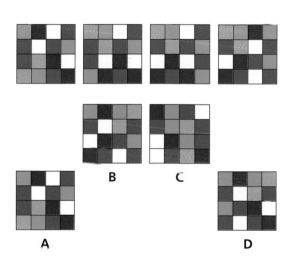

B

C

A

D

At first glance the stained-glass windows in St. Confused's Church seem entirely random. But window expert Dr. C. Threw spots a pattern. Which one of the windows here is the next in the sequence?

Wondrous Windows - Solution

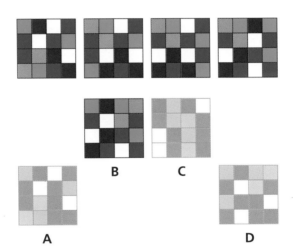

B

C

A

D

Each time, half of the window is flipped
round lengthways (as if the glass was taken out and put
back in back-to-front) ~ first the left-hand half, then the
bottom half, then the right-hand half, and so on
proceeding anti-clockwise around the window shape.

Mat-imatics

Rating 2 Points

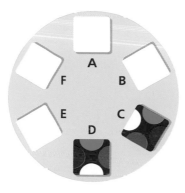

A set of six table mats features coloured shapes
as shown. All the mats display the combination
of colours in a different order and are all different
to each other. The mats are placed on a circular
table with the colours on the sides of mats that are
next to each other, moving from one place to the
next, being the same. All four colours appear at
least once on the inner and outer sides as they appear
on the table. In fact there are 3 green shapes on
the outer sides and 3 yellow shapes on the inner sides.
John can see the mat in front of him and to
his right. What does the mat opposite him look like?

Mat-imatics - Solution

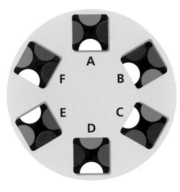

The mat opposite John is A and the mats
on the table are laid out as shown.

Cosmic Coins

Rating 2 Points

4 ○ = 1 ▲

3 ▲ = 1 ✴

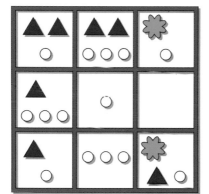

In the currency system of the planet Helix, four ogs make up one plunket and there are three plunkets in a zap. Work out the sequence and find out which coins should be in the empty space.

Cosmic Coins - Solution

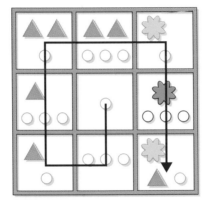

One zap and three ogs. The sequence runs
1, 3, 5, 7, 9 etc. in the above pattern around the grid.

All Aboard

Rating 3 Points

- **HILL STREET BUS STATION**
- Rye Road
- The Wood
- Queen's Hall
- King's Theatre
- Levens Close
- Kirby Square
- Town Hall Square
- Gilbody Place
- The Stadium
- Market Cross
- Tollington Drive
- Westgate
- Heather Green
- Murdoch House
- Rose Villas

Suzy has accidentally caught the X66, an express bus that doesn't stop at all the bus stops along its route. She wants to get off at Murdoch House. Will she be able to?

All Aboard - Solution

● **HILL STREET BUS STATION**

Rye Road
● **The Wood**
● **Queen's Hall**

King's Theatre
Levens Close
Kirby Square
● **Town Hall Square**

Gilbody Place
The Stadium
● **Market Cross**
● **Tollington Drive**

Westgate
● **Heather Green**

Murdoch House
● **Rose Villas**

No. The X66 only stops at places
with a double letter in their name.

Parachute Drop

Rating 1 Point

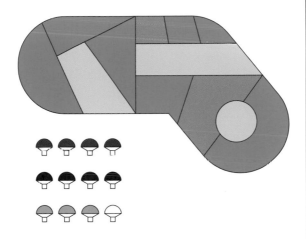

Farmer Jones has kindly allowed 12 parachutists to land in his fields, provided that only one parachute lands in each field, and that no two parachutes of the same colour end up in adjoining fields. The parachutists have 4 red parachutes, 4 black parachutes, 3 blue parachutes and 1 yellow parachute. Can they all land in Farmer Jones' fields and keep to his rules?

Parachute Drop - Solution

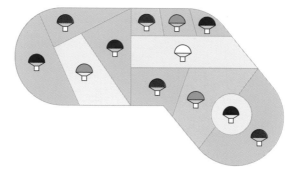

This is one way they could drop.

Against the Odds

Rating 2 Points

White is moving up the board. It is his move. Black is
threatening to mate him - in five different ways!
Can White still draw?

Against the Odds - Solution

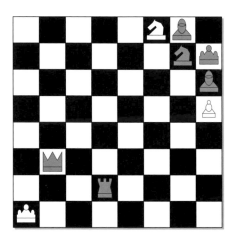

White moves the advanced pawn forward and promotes it to a knight, giving check. The black king is forced to move into the corner, then the white knight moves back to check the king again. Then the white knight continues to give check indefinitely, securing a draw by perpetual check (1 Pf8=N check Kh8 2 Ng6 check Kh7 3 Nf8 check, etc.). This is the only way to draw - if White takes the bishop, giving check by a new queen, Black recaptures it with his own queen, avoiding stalemate.

Weights in the Wood

Rating 1 Point

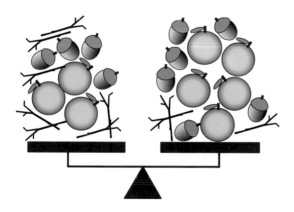

Professor Beechnut collects a bucketful of
botanical samples in Waverley Wood. With the
following information, can you help him uncover more
knowledge? 4 acorns, 3 apples and 7 twigs weigh the
same as 6 acorns, 5 apples and 3 twigs.
An apple is 3 times heavier than an acorn.
There are 20 twigs in a kilogram (2.2lbs).
How heavy is an apple?

Weights in the Wood - Solution

 = 75g

An apple weighs 75g (2.64oz).

Ray of Light

Rating 1 Point

How many triangles are there
altogether in this pattern?

Ray of Light - Solution

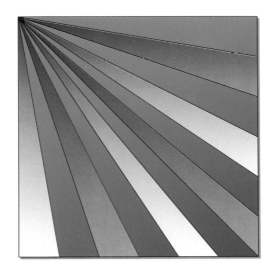

42.

Arrow Maze

Rating 2 Points

Find your way through this
maze from left to right.

Arrow Maze - Solution

Circular Computations

Rating 2 Points

11, 12, 19, 23, 34, 43, 45, 55, 58.

Place three numbers in each third of the circle, with one of them in the Inner circle, so that the three numbers in each third all add up to 100, AND so that the three numbers in the inner circle also add up to 100.

Circular Computations - Solution

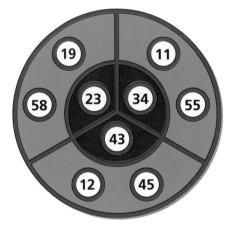

Jigsaw Jewel

Rating 1 Point

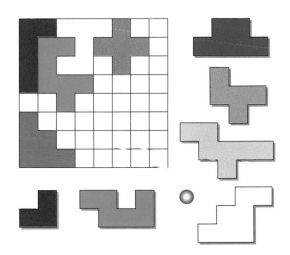

Helen is completing a puzzle and has
these remaining pieces to fit in. The smallest
piece of the puzzle is a precious stone that takes
up only one square. Which square will it go in?

Jigsaw Jewel - Solution

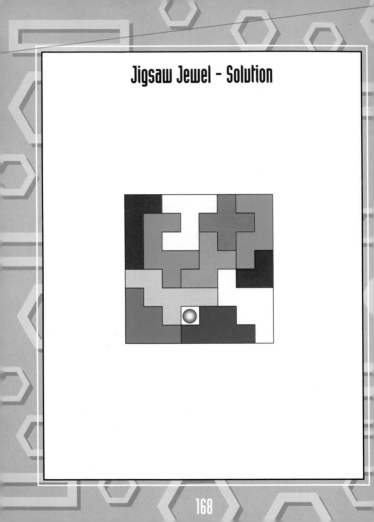

Bathroom Tiles

Rating 3 Points

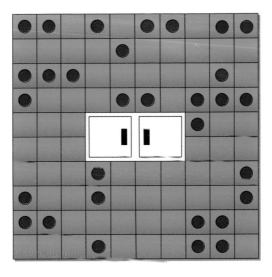

According to the sequence, what pattern of tiles lies behind the cabinet on this bathroom wall?

Bathroom Tiles - Solution

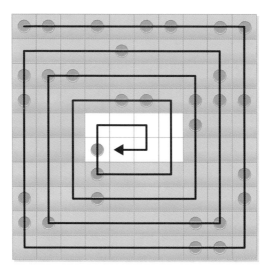

The sequence runs in the spiral pattern shown here.
The pattern of: Two dots - space - one dot - space -
two dots - space is repeated but in each cycle the
number of spaces is increased by one.

TV Crew

Rating 3 Points

MONDAY	Reg	Richard	Rowena
TUESDAY	Reg	Rowena	Richard
WEDNESDAY	Rowena	Reg	Richard
THURSDAY	Rowena	Richard	Reg

The three presenters on Nightly News agree to sit in different positions each night so that no one looks more important than the others. They also agree to wear different coloured outfits from each other on every show. If the same sequence continues, where will they be sitting and what colours will they be wearing on Friday?

TV Crew - Solution

Richard

Rowena

Reg

Each presenter rotates seats staying two nights if sitting on the end of a row and one night if sitting in the middle. The colours, meanwhile, follow the same pattern.

Number Chain

Rating 2 Points

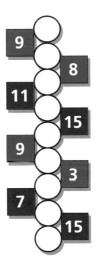

Place the digits 1 to 9 in the circles so
that the numbers within the two circles touching
each square add to the total in that square.

Number Chain - Solution

Pathfinder Puzzle

Rating 2 Points

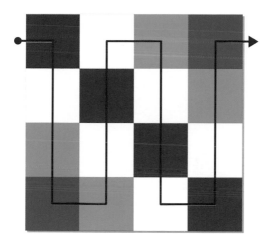

The puzzle above shows a path from the top
left-hand corner to the top right hand corner
of a four by four grid of tiles.
How many other different routes could there be,
going through all sixteen tiles once only,
to enter and exit at the same places?

Pathfinder Puzzle - Solution

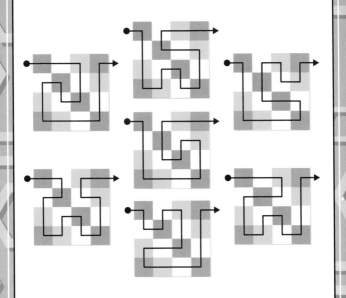

There are seven other possible routes.

Odd One Out

Rating 3 Points

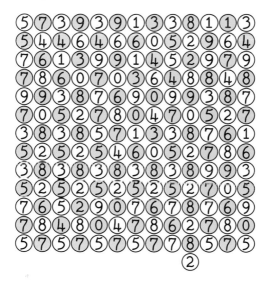

In this maze you must start at the bottom and make your way upwards from number to number. However, you can only move over the even numbers.

Odd One Out - Solution

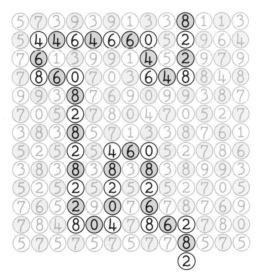

12-Card Turnover

Rating 1 Point

6 ♣	9 ♦	7 ♥
J ♦	8 ♣	10 ♠
9 ♥	?	10 ♣
A ♠	J ♥	K ♦

Work out the sequence and name
the overturned card.

12-Card Turnover - Solution

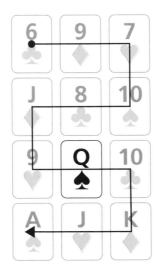

Queen of spades.
The sequence runs in the pattern shown here.
The numbers go up 3 and down 2, up 3 and down 2,
and so on. Meanwhile the trumps cycle in alphabetical
order: clubs, diamonds, hearts, spades.

Maple Mystery Maze

Rating 2 Points

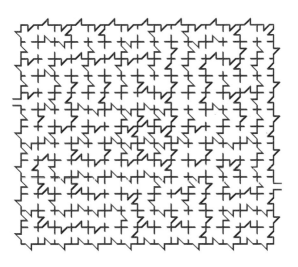

Find a path from the left-hand-side
of the maze that takes you through
the labyrinth of leaves until you reach
the exit on the right.

Maple Mystery Maze - Solution

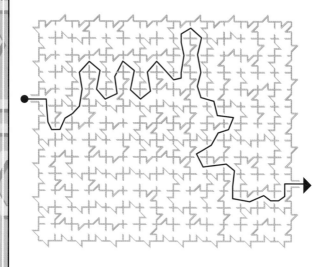

Egg Box Enigma

Rating 3 Points

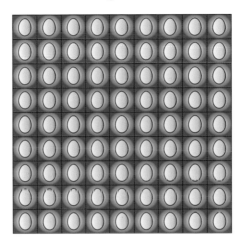

Erika has a square box of 81 eggs (9 rows with 9 eggs in each row). She needs to make a very large omelette, but she can't bear to leave an unsymmetrical pattern of eggs in the box. "In fact," says Erika, "not only do I want the pattern to be symmetrical when viewed from any corner or any side, but I want there to be 16 rows of eggs with five eggs in each row!" Can such a pattern be made with the remaining 33 eggs?

Egg Box Enigma - Solution

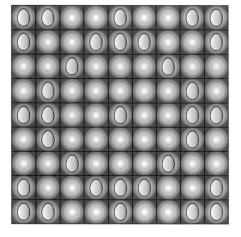

Cup Challenge

Rating 2 Points

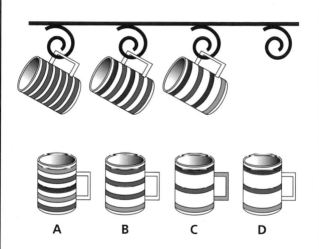

A   B   C   D

Which cup belongs on the empty hook?

Cup Challenge - Solution

Each time, the number of stripes goes down 1,
but the number of colours used in all goes up 1.

Field Work

Rating 1 Point

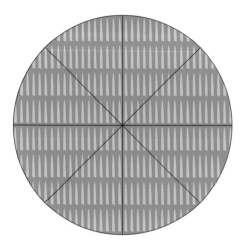

Professor Beechnut is taking 11 of his students
on a botanical field trip. He wants to divide a circular field
into 11 sections, so everyone can have a section to study.
But he only has four straight dividers with which to do it.
The professor can only manage to make 8 sections,
arranging the dividers like this. But swotty Stella
says she can make 11. How does she do it?

Field Work - Solution

Houndstooth Maze

Rating 3 Points

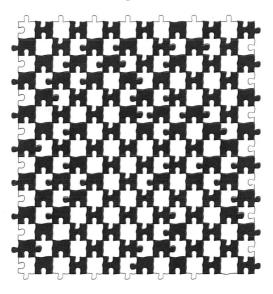

Move from one puzzle piece to the next,
where they do not interlock, i.e. along
straight edges only, to get from the
top to the bottom of this maze.

Houndstooth Maze - Solution

Overall Scoring Page

CHAPTER	SCORE CARD	POTENTIAL SCORE	YOUR SCORE
1	Page 8	**40**	_____
2	Page 54	**40**	_____
3	Page 100	**45**	_____
4	Page 146	**45**	_____
		GRAND TOTAL	___

*Any one who has got 128 points or above
can afford to sit back and feel smug – congratulations
you've got a score in the top quartile!*

*Any one who has between 85 and 128 points
should feel reasonably happy with his or
her score having got more than half of
the puzzles (and they are difficult!) correct.*

*Those with less than 85 points, however, should
turn over to page 192 for more information on our
other Brain-Boosting titles – you need more practice!*

OTHER BRAIN-BOOSTING TITLES AVAILABLE
FROM LAGOON BOOKS

Brain Boosting Visual Logic Puzzles
ISBN 1902813200

Brain Boosting Cryptic Puzzles
ISBN 1902813219

Brain Boosting Lateral Thinking Puzzles
ISBN 1902813227

Brain Boosting Sequence Puzzles
ISBN 1902813537

Brain Boosting Quantum Puzzles
ISBN 1902813529

Brain Boosting Cryptology Puzzles
ISBN 1902813545

You can view our full range of puzzle books along
with the full collection of Lagoon Books on our website

www.lagoongames.com

**LAGOON
BOOKS**